THE

Easter

CODE

A 40-DAY
JOURNEY TO THE CROSS

O. S. Hawkins

COUNTRYMAN ®

A Division of Thomas Nelson Publishers

THOMAS NELSON
Since 1798

Published in Nashville, Tennessee, by Thomas Nelson. Thomas Nelson is a registered trademark of HarperCollins Christian Publishing, Inc.

Thomas Nelson titles may be purchased in bulk for educational, business, fund-raising, or sales promotional use. For information, please e-mail SpecialMarkets@ThomasNelson.com.

ISBN-13: 978-1-4002-1148-7

Printed in the United States

18 19 20 21 22 POL 6 5 4 3 2 1

INTRODUCTION

A sh Wednesday begins the Lenten season for millions of professing Christians around the world. It is marked by a period of self-denial during which adherents, for the forty days leading up to the celebration of Easter, will endeavor to "give up" something for God. Many observers believe that "giving something up" for Lent is the path to pleasing God. But the Bible clearly teaches that grace can never be earned, for it is the "gift of God, not of works" (Ephesians 2:8–9).

The Easter Code is a call to freedom during the days of Lent. As we focus on repentance of sin and consecration of ourselves afresh and anew to God, it is a reminder that this is a 365-day-a-year discipline, and not simply a 40-day period of testing. We are called to a lifestyle of dedication and discipline. Remember: we are cleansed and made pure only through the shed blood of the Lord Jesus Christ, not through any feeble attempt of our own to please a holy God. While fasting, abstinence, and self-denial are worthy goals for all believers, they can never bring us into favor with God apart from His unmerited grace upon us. Salvation is not about guilt. It is all about grace!

In the pages of devotions that follow, we will be walking with Jesus along the journey to Jerusalem. Matthew records, "From that time Jesus began to show to His disciples that *He must go to Jerusalem*, and suffer many things from the elders and chief priests and scribes, and be killed, and be raised on the third day" (Matthew 16:21, emphasis added). Along this journey with Jesus we will be visiting *places* He went, *people* with whom He spoke, *parables* He told along the way, *promises* He left for all posterity, and the powerful and expressive *prayers* He offered.

The journey to Jerusalem culminates on a Roman cross outside the city walls of Jerusalem, but it doesn't end there! This is why in our evangelical world we do not use the symbol of the crucifix but always an empty cross to signify that death and the grave could not hold Jesus down. He arose, the ever-living Lord and Savior.

While traditional Lenten devotionals omit the Sundays from Ash Wednesday to Easter and consist of forty devotions, *The Easter Code* consists of forty-two, including Palm Sunday and Easter Sunday, with its promise of the second chance. Each devotion contains a devotional thought, a "code word" for the day, a Scripture, and a daily prayer. The code word helps unlock the blessing of each day's reading. Write it down, keep it with you, and ponder its meaning. Claim the Scripture as your very own, climb upon it, and stand there throughout the day. Make the daily prayer a part of your own walk with Christ as you repeat it often.

Now it is time to begin this great adventure of walking with Christ daily . . . on our own "journey to Jerusalem"!

ASH WEDNESDAY

As we journey through this day in the normal traffic patterns of our lives, we will see men and women with ashes in the form of a cross on their foreheads. It is a visible reminder on this Ash Wednesday that "dust [we] are, and to dust [we] shall return" (Genesis 3:19). Today begins a period of fasting and self-denial. It is a good reminder that the only way to please God is not by what we do—or refrain from doing—but by accepting His gracious offer of forgiveness made possible through Christ's shed blood on the cross.

Salvation is God's work, not our work. "For by grace you have been saved" (Ephesians 2:8a). Our salvation begins with Jesus—not with us. It is not His response to any good works we may do or evil works from which we've refrained. Salvation is provided for us wholly because of His grace, His unmerited favor toward you and me. The Father did not send His only Son to die for our sins because we kept begging and pleading for Him to do so. It was by His grace alone.

Salvation is God's work in God's way, not our way. It is "through faith . . . not of yourselves; it is the gift of God" (Ephesians 2:8b). I want to shout those words on this Ash Wednesday—"Through faith . . . not of yourselves . . . not of works!" No amount of doing good deeds or abstaining from certain pleasures can earn God's favor. Salvation is wholly by grace, through our faith in Christ alone . . . God's gift to us.

CODE WORD: DONE

No matter what you do or don't do, or what you give or give up, your salvation is not spelled D-O but D-O-N-E! Today remember that Christ paid a huge price to redeem you. It is already done! Your part is to receive this gift by faith.

A PASSION PROCLAMATION

[It is] not by works of righteousness which we have done, but according to His mercy He saved us.

TITUS 3:5

. . . .

Lord, thank You for giving me what I never deserved—grace! And for Your mercy in not giving me what I do deserve. No wonder we call it "amazing grace"! In Jesus' name, amen.

DAY 1: THURSDAY

*R*epentance has become one of the forgotten words in our English vocabulary. Yet it was the message of all the prophets. It was the message John the Baptist preached in the Jordan Valley. It was the message of Jesus as He commenced His ministry, saying, "Repent, for the kingdom of heaven is at hand" (Matthew 4:17). It was the message that birthed the church at Pentecost and the message of all the apostles. The Lenten season begins with a call to repent for each of us.

But what really is behind this word? Repentance is not remorse, being sorry for our sin. The rich young ruler went away "sorrowful" but didn't repent (Matthew 19:16–22). It is not simply regret, wishing that some moment could be lived over again. Pilate washed his hands, regretting his evil deed, but he didn't repent (Matthew 27:24). Repentance is not reform, that is, trying to turn over a new leaf. Judas reformed by returning the silver coins of betrayal but didn't repent (Matthew 27:3).

Repentance emerges from a Greek word meaning "to change one's mind," which results in a change of will, which in turn results in a change of action. While repentance begins with a change of mind, the real proof will be found in a change of attitude and action.

CODE WORD: CHANGE

Begin today to change your mind about your *sin*. It is not some vice to be laughed off. Sin is so serious it necessitated the cross. Also change your mind about your *self*. You cannot please God through self-righteousness. Finally, change your mind about your *Savior*. Jesus is not just some teacher or prophet, but He is God, who clothed Himself in human flesh and gave Himself for you.

A PASSION PROCLAMATION

Repent . . . , that your sins may be blotted out, so that times of refreshing may come from the presence of the Lord.

ACTS 3:16

Lord, I can't excuse my sin by claiming everyone else is doing it, nor can I minimize it by asserting it is not as bad as someone else's. I confess: I have sinned against You, and I am wholly dependent on Your grace and mercy. In Jesus' name, amen.

DAY 2: FRIDAY

The essence of biblical repentance is beautifully embedded in the old and often-repeated story of the prodigal son. The young man found himself not only broke—having left his family home and spent his inheritance—but broken. While feeding swine in a pigpen, he actually longed for the husks they were eating, and he "came to himself" (Luke 15:17). This first step in the repentance process, this change of mind, brought about the second step, a change in his will, his volition. In the next verse he exclaimed, "I will arise and go to my father." Once his mind and will were changed, his actions were sure to follow. Thus we read, "He arose and came to his father" (v. 20).

Repentance is a change of mind. That is it! And how do we know that we have truly changed our minds? Our volition will be changed as well, and our changed actions—resulting in a new life direction—will follow as naturally as water running downhill.

Repentance and faith are inseparable, born at the same time. They are two sides of the same coin. Repentance alone will not get you to heaven, but you can't get there without it. No wonder Jesus said, "Repent, for the kingdom of heaven is at hand" (Matthew 4:17).

CODE WORD: PROBE

Ask God today to bring to the surface of your heart and mind that thing that displeases Him and for which you need to repent. Then change your mind about it, and your will and actions will follow.

A PASSION PROCLAMATION

Search me, O God, and know my heart . . .
See if there is any wicked way in me, and
lead me in the way everlasting.

PSALM 139:23–24

. . . .

Lord, I am willing; I am willing to be made willing! Grant to me repentance and faith today. I throw myself upon Your mercy and stand in Your grace. In Jesus' name, amen.

I love the way the apostle Paul framed the subject of repentance: "The goodness of God leads you to repentance" (Romans 2:4). Once, when our daughters were small, my wife and I rented a vacation home deep in the Smoky Mountains. That first night in that strange place was, as author and educator James Weldon Johnson put it, "blacker than a hundred midnights down in a cypress swamp"![1]

I was awakened in the middle of the night by the cries of our little seven-year-old at the top of the stairs. I bounded up the stairs to find her disoriented and scared in the darkness. I took her by the hand and led her down the stairs into the security of our own bed, where she soundly slept the rest of the night away.

And so it is that our dear Lord finds us in the night, often disoriented by the issues of life. He takes us by the hand, and, as the Bible says, His own goodness "leads [us] to repentance."

When all is said and done, what difference will it make if we drive luxury cars, eat vitamin-enriched foods, live in palatial homes, and are buried in mahogany caskets if we rise up in judgment to meet a God we do not know? Let His goodness take you by the hand today. He will lead you to repentance.

CODE WORD: HAND

It may be that for too long you have called all the shots. Put your hand in His hand today. Go ahead, do it. He will lead you to repentance.

A PASSION PROCLAMATION

The goodness of God leads you to repentance.

Romans 2:4

. . . .

Lord, I am amazed at Your love for me. You are a good God, and I put my hand in Yours today. Lead me in the way I should go. In Jesus' name, amen.

DAY 4: MONDAY

The Bible says, "And the Word became flesh and dwelt among us" (John 1:14). Who is this "Word"? It is God Himself, stepping out of heaven, clothing Himself in human flesh, and physically invading human history. John leaves no doubt concerning this identity: "In the beginning was the Word, and the Word was with God, and *the Word was God*" (John 1:1, emphasis added).

Jesus came down to where we are so that we could one day go to where He is! He came not clinging to the brightness of His glory, not shunning us for our sinful condition, but humbling Himself and taking on a garment of flesh. By doing so He can say to you and me, no matter our emotional condition, temptations, or pain, "I understand."

He "dwelt among us, . . . full of grace and truth" (John 1:14). Jesus is full of grace. Because of His sacrifice, we don't get what we deserve, and that is called grace. And He is full of truth. It is only when His grace leads us to know the truth that we are truly free.

But that is not all. "We beheld His glory" (John 1:14). Paul said it like this: "Christ in you, the hope of glory" (Colossians 1:27). Have you personally beheld His glory *in you*?

CODE WORD: CONDESCENSION

When Jesus came and took on flesh, it was one of the most amazing acts of condescension to be found anywhere at any time. As you think of this code word today, marvel at how much you mean to Him.

A PASSION PROCLAMATION

"I will not leave you comfortless: I will come to you."

JOHN 14:18 KJV

. . . .

Lord, You humbled Yourself in coming to earth so I could go to heaven. And one day, because of Your marvelous grace, I can go to where You are because You came to where I am. In Jesus' name, amen.

DAY 5: TUESDAY

We had a really good start. Life began in a perfect paradise. The climate was never too warm and never too cold. We had no heartaches, no worries. We felt no aches or pains. We were doing wonderfully well—*until* we disobeyed and ate the forbidden fruit and were expelled from the garden.

The first evidence of this demise came when Adam and Eve saw "that they were naked" (Genesis 3:7). They had been naked all along, but not until sin came did they take their eyes off God and put them on themselves. This is always what sin does. Before, God had been the center of their attention and devotion. Sin entered the picture, and their focus became centered squarely upon themselves.

Their first impulse? Grab some fig leaves and cover their nakedness. But God in His grace intervened because all the human mechanisms we use to try and cover our sin never suffice. He took an innocent little animal, killed it, and covered Adam and Eve with its skin. When that animal breathed its last breath, it became the first to know the expensive toll that sin takes on one's life.

God placed our first parents in a perfect paradise. We fell. God drove us out. And you and I have been trying to get back into His presence ever since. The account begins with paradise lost in Genesis and ends with paradise regained in Revelation. Right now we are exiles from Eden. But we are making our way back home through the substitutionary sacrifice of Jesus Christ.

CODE WORD: SACRIFICE

"Without [the] shedding of blood there is no remission [of sin]" (Hebrews 9:22). Just as a sacrificial animal covered the sins of Adam and Eve, so the sacrifice of Christ on the cross is the only covering for our own sin.

A PASSION PROCLAMATION

"The one who comes to Me I will by no means cast out."

John 6:37

. . . .

Lord, I come to You now admitting I can do nothing in and of myself to cleanse my sin. I trust today in Your shed blood to cover me and cleanse me. Hosanna!

The Old Testament conceals Christ. The New Testament reveals Him! And there is no more vivid and visual foreshadowing of His substitutionary sacrifice for your sin than is found in the account of Abraham's sacrifice of his own son Isaac (Genesis 22:1–14).

God had promised Abraham he would be the father of a great nation. There was only one problem: he and his wife were old, beyond childbearing age, and his wife, Sarah, had spent a lifetime unable to conceive (see Genesis 17). And then they got their miracle: Isaac was born!

This was all too quickly followed by a time of testing: "Take now your son, your only son Isaac, whom you love . . . and offer him . . . as a burnt offering on one of the mountains of which I shall tell you" (Genesis 22:2).

Along the journey up Mount Moriah, the lad asked, "Father, where is the lamb for the sacrifice?" Abraham responded in faith, "The Lord will provide the lamb" (paraphrase of Genesis 22:7–8)

In obedience to God, Abraham built the altar and placed his son upon it. And just at the right time God was faithful to His word: "Then Abraham lifted his eyes and looked, and there behind him was a ram caught in a thicket by its horns. So Abraham went and took the ram, and offered it up for a burnt offering instead of his son. And Abraham called the name of the place, The-Lord-Will-Provide; as it is said to this day" (vv. 13–14).

CODE WORD: PICTURE

Today as you look at a picture on your desk or on your phone, let it be a reminder to you of this beautiful picture of Christ taking your place, dying your death, so you can live His life today!

A PASSION PROCLAMATION

But without faith it is impossible to please Him, for he who comes to God must believe that He is, and that He is a rewarder of those who diligently seek Him.

HEBREWS 11:6

Lord, what You promise You are faithful to provide. Like Abraham, I wait in faith, believing You to do "exceeding abundantly above all" I might ask or think.[2] In Jesus' name, amen.

On our journey to Jerusalem, we find another poignant picture of our coming Savior when we arrive at Exodus 12. One of the most important dates on the calendar of our Jewish friends is the evening they celebrate the Passover seder meal commemorating their freedom from death and deliverance from Egyptian bondage. God had sent a series of plagues on Egypt, where God's people were enslaved. The most devastating plague came on the night the death angel passed over every home in Egypt, bringing death to the firstborn of every family.

The Jews were instructed to take a little lamb, perfect and without blemish, slay it, and spread the blood over the doorposts of their homes so that when the death angel came, he would "see the blood" and "pass over" that particular residence (Exodus 12:13). The firstborn in those homes would be saved by the blood of the sacrificed lamb.

It is no wonder that fifteen hundred years later, when Jesus burst forth from the obscurity of the carpenter's shop and appeared in the Jordan Valley, John the Baptist pointed an index finger in His direction and shouted, "Behold! The Lamb of God who takes away the sin of the world!" (John 1:29). Would you, today, take a moment and behold the Lamb for yourself?

⁌⟡⁍

CODE WORD: FREEDOM

The sacrifice of the Lamb of God, the Lord Jesus, is what brings true freedom to your soul. Freedom is never free. It is always bought with blood. Rejoice today in the freedom Christ brings. God is not looking for human effort. He is looking to see if you have applied the blood of Christ to the door of your heart.

A PASSION PROCLAMATION

The blood of Jesus Christ [God's]
Son cleanses us from all sin.

1 JOHN 1:7

. . . .

"Dear dying Lamb, Your precious blood shall never lose its power, till all the ransomed church of God be saved, to sin no more."[3] *Hallelujah!*

DAY 8: FRIDAY

Many of the recorded psalms of David point to the coming Messiah. There is a strong messianic appeal in his probing question in Psalm 24: "Who may ascend into the hill of the LORD? Or, who may stand in His holy place?" (v. 3). Quick comes the answer: "He who has clean hands and a pure heart" (v. 4). That leaves me out, and I am pretty sure you as well.

My hands, representing my outward life, are not clean. And my inner life, my heart, is far from being pure. Like everyone's, my "heart is deceitful above all things, and desperately wicked" (Jeremiah 17:9).

How will we ever be able to ascend this hill, much less stand in God's holy place? There is only one who has walked this way and meets these two criteria: the Lord Jesus, the King of glory. His hands were clean and His heart was pure. Thus, knowing we were without hope, He came and His hands became dirty with the sin of the world, your sin and mine. And His pure heart became sin for us. Why? His clean hands became dirty so my dirty hands could become clean. His pure heart took my sin so my impure heart could become pure.

One day we will hear again the words from this psalm saying, "Lift up your heads, O you gates"

(Psalm 24:7), and a multitude that no one can number will arrive with our King at the gate of heaven . . . and the King of glory will come in, accompanied by everyone who looked to Him in faith for their eternal salvation.

CODE WORD: GATE

Today when you see or pass through a gate, let it remind you that the only way you will enter into the gate of heaven is through the Lord Jesus Christ. He is the door through which we enter in.

A PASSION PROCLAMATION

"Blessed are the pure in heart for they shall see God."

MATTHEW 5:8

Lord, I open wide the gate of my heart to You today. "Come in. Come in today. Come in to stay. Come into my heart, Lord Jesus."[4] Amen.

DAY 9: SATURDAY

Throughout the Old Testament we see foreshadows of the coming, promised Messiah. This week along the journey to Jerusalem, we have seen them in Genesis, Exodus, and the Psalms. As the sun of God's revelation to man continues to rise, we find it casting a perfect shadow when we arrive at Isaiah 53. This is, without question, one of the most vibrant pictures of our coming Lord to be found anywhere.

Isaiah, hundreds of years before Christ, framed it like this:

> He is despised and rejected by men, a Man of sorrows and acquainted with grief. And we hid, as it were, our faces from Him; He was despised, and we did not esteem Him. Surely He has borne our griefs and carried our sorrows; yet we esteemed Him stricken, smitten by God, and afflicted. But He was wounded for our transgressions, He was bruised for our iniquities; the chastisement for our peace was upon Him, and by His stripes we are healed. All we like sheep have gone astray; we have turned, every one, to his own way; and the LORD has laid on Him the iniquity of us all. (Isaiah 53:3–6)

He was wounded for our transgressions, though He never transgressed. He was bruised for our iniquities, though He never knew iniquity. And when we had all gone our own way, God took your sin, my sin, and "laid on Him the iniquity of us all." He took your sin so you today can take on His righteousness.

CODE WORD: SHEEP

Sheep can't be trained. They are also directionless and defenseless, not prepared for flight or fight. That is you and me. Like sheep, we have gone our way, but thankfully, the Lord laid on Christ the sins of us all.

A PASSION PROCLAMATION

For He made Him who knew no sin to be sin for us, that we might become the righteousness of God in Him.

2 CORINTHIANS 5:21

. . . .

Lord, I don't always know the right way to go. I am so often defenseless. You are my Shepherd. Lead me today in the way You would have me go; I will follow. In Jesus' name, amen.

Jesus' own physical journey to Jerusalem began when He invaded human history in the form of a baby in the quiet little village of Bethlehem. Christ's genealogy reads, "And Jacob begot Joseph the husband of Mary, of whom was born Jesus who is called Christ" (Matthew 1:16). After an exhaustive list of names, each of whom "begot" the next, the line of "begots" ends here. Note it does not say that "Joseph begot Jesus." And for good reason. This was a virgin birth. The "whom" in Greek is feminine singular, referring only to Mary. In her teenage womb, God the Father implanted the seed of His only begotten Son. Hundreds of years earlier, Isaiah had foretold that this would be the "sign" of the long-awaited Messiah—the virgin birth (Isaiah 7:14)!

It is because Jesus was Mary's "seed" (see Genesis 3:15) and not the seed of Joseph that entitles Him to be the one and only, unique Son of God, Savior of the world. The virgin birth is the bedrock of His authority and our salvation.

CODE WORD: SIGN

As you go about your day today and see a hundred different signs seeking to grab your attention, let it remind you that without the virgin birth our Lord could never be the promised Messiah, your sin-bearer . . . your Savior.

A PASSION PROCLAMATION

The LORD Himself will give you a sign;
behold, the virgin shall conceive and bear a
Son, and shall call His name Immanuel.

ISAIAH 7:14

. . . .

Lord, You are not God and man. You and You
alone are the unique God-Man. Thank You for
coming in flesh so You can understand my every
need and meet it today. In Jesus' name, amen.

DAY 11: TUESDAY

Because of the adoration afforded Mary from our Catholic and Orthodox friends, I often wonder if we, in our evangelical world, sometimes fail to give her the honor she is due. After the pain, sweat, and contractions of birthing the Christ child in a stable, she got up from her makeshift straw pallet, wrapped the babe in cloths, and "laid Him in a manger" (Luke 2:7). How moving are those words!

Mary held all these things to herself and she "pondered them in her heart" (v. 19). She was putting it all together, weighing in her mind the long-held Jewish prophecies of a coming Messiah, the angel's message nine months earlier, the visit of the angelic choir that starlit night.

She never stopped pondering these things in her heart. And thirty-three years later, she was there at the cross, feeling the pain and loss that only a mother can feel over her son. She knew all along that the finer things of life would never be His; that He would be despised and rejected with no place to lay His head. But He was destined for greater things: giving sight to the blind and healing to the sick, only to finally feel the pain of being pierced with cruel Roman iron spikes. Yes, she knew. She pondered. She was there.

And she was there three days later when He arose, the living Lord and Savior!

CODE WORD: COOK

The word "ponder" in Greek means to mix together as a cook would stir together different ingredients in a bowl. When you cook your next meal, let it remind you to "ponder" all the things God has done and is doing in your life today.

A PASSION PROCLAMATION

"Well done, good and faithful servant; you have been faithful over a few things, I will make you ruler over many things. Enter into the joy of your lord."

MATTHEW 25:23

Lord, help me see today that even though everything that happens in my life may not seem good, You take it all, stir it up, and make it all work for my good and Your glory. In Jesus' name, amen.

One of the forgotten figures along Jesus' own journey to Jerusalem was one of the most important ones as well. When it came time for God the Father to pick a man to mentor and raise His own son, He chose Joseph. And for thirty years Jesus lived under his roof as God was preparing Him for a ministry that would last only three years but was destined to change the entire course of human history.

The Bible records not a syllable that ever left Joseph's lips. Virtually everyone in the narrative of Christ is quoted *except* Joseph. At Christmastime we sing traditional carols of almost everyone who appears in the Christmas story: Mary, the shepherds, the wise men, the angels, even the star . . . but not Joseph. No one seems to sing about him even at Christmas.

But there is a reason God chose this man. Joseph was faithful. Always. When the angel came to Joseph in a dream with the message that his fiancée was pregnant but that he should not fear to take her as his wife, he believed it, knowing he would become the brunt of every joke in his hometown. When the angel told him to leave Bethlehem to save the babe from Herod's decree to kill the baby boys of Bethlehem, there was no doubt, no defiance, no delay.

Our legacy from this good man was not found in

what he said; it is found in what really matters: what he did! The entire Christmas narrative hinges on Joseph's faithfulness.

CODE WORD: ORDINARY

God still has a way of choosing ordinary people just like you and me. Learn a lesson from another one of us: Joseph, a common carpenter. God still uses ordinary people and then does extraordinary things through their faithfulness and obedience.

A PASSION PROCLAMATION

God has chosen the foolish things of the world to . . . shame [confound] the wise . . . that no flesh should glory in His presence.

1 CORINTHIANS 1:27, 29

Lord, keep me ever mindful today that when it feels as if no one cares, listens, or watches me, You do! Your eyes are upon the righteous, and Your ears attend to my prayers. In Jesus' name, amen.

DAY 13: THURSDAY

One of the most misquoted verses in all the Bible is found in Revelation when John, in his letter to the church at Ephesus, makes this accusation: "You have left your first love" (Revelation 2:4). Ask a hundred people who may have heard of this verse and the majority will remember it as saying, "You have lost your first love." But there is a world of difference in admitting that we left something and having to admit we lost something. The admission that "I left something" seems to carry more personal responsibility than simply saying, "I lost something."

Mary and Joseph could relate to leaving something. They had gone on an annual pilgrimage with twelve-year-old Jesus to Jerusalem and were returning home. Since Jesus was still a child, He could have traveled in the men's caravan or the women's. As Jesus' parents came to the end of the first day's journey, they realized He was not with either of them. It was not until they admitted they had not *lost* Him but *left* Him back in Jerusalem that they found Him—right there at the temple, in dialogue with the elders (Luke 2:42–49).

On your own journey to Jerusalem, could it be that you didn't "lose" your first love after all . . . you *left* Him? Go back to where you left Jesus, and you, like Mary and Joseph, will find Him right there.

CODE WORD: LOST

If you are like me, most of the times when you think you lost something, the truth is, you left it somewhere. Let this be a reminder that we can never lose our love for Christ, although we may leave it from time to time.

A PASSION PROCLAMATION

Be strong and of good courage, do not fear nor be afraid . . . for the LORD your God, He is the One who goes with you. He will not leave you nor forsake you.

DEUTERONOMY 31:6

Lord, You are faithful. When I feel an estrangement, it is never because You have moved or left me. It is because I am the one who left my first love. Thank You for always being near. In Jesus' name, amen.

DAY 14: FRIDAY

During His intense struggle on the cross, our Lord spoke seven times as He hung suspended between heaven and earth. The strangest of these cries was, "My God, My God, why have You forsaken Me?" (Matthew 27:46). Along the journey to Jerusalem, He knew well what it was to be forsaken. In Galilee He was forsaken by His family. They distanced themselves from Him, and we read that He had no honor "in his own house" (Matthew 13:57). In Gethsemane He was forsaken by His friends when they ran away after He was taken by the mob (Mark 14:50). And at the end of the journey, at Golgotha, while bearing our sins, He was forsaken for a time by His Father so that we might never be forsaken.

Perhaps there is no more haunting word in our entire English language than the word *forsaken*. Many today know this haunting reality. There are those who one day stood at a wedding altar, hearing the loves of their life promise to "never leave or forsake" them. But they lied and left the gnawing pain of being forsaken. Countless children, abandoned by their fathers and/ or mothers, also know the meaning of this cruel word.

Jesus truly knew its meaning. But He didn't give up. He reached up! This is a help and a hope for any of us who have been forsaken. He understands. Don't give up. Reach up.

CODE WORD: UP

So many times, when difficulties or heartbreak come knocking on our door, we look at the swirling circumstances around us, or worse, focus all our attention on them. But look up. Be reminded that Jesus sees a sparrow that falls to the ground and cares much more for you.

A PASSION PROCLAMATION

When my father and my mother forsake me,
*then the L*ORD *will take care of me.*

PSALM 27:10

Lord, I am so grateful that there is no fear of You ever forsaking me. I stand on Your promise that You will never leave or forsake me . . . ever. In Jesus' name, amen.

DAY 15: SATURDAY

That fateful night before the crucifixion, Jesus needed His friends and followers more than ever before. But on the heels of His agonizing prayer in Gethsemane's garden, He was seized by the mob. The Bible rather bluntly states, "All the disciples forsook Him and fled" (Matthew 26:56). All of them forsook Him in His greatest hour of need. But that is not all; they fled. They ran away into the darkness, some denying that they had ever known Him. And to make matters worse, this was not the action of His foes, but His friends.

There is a life lesson here for all of us. Instead of just giving in, Jesus made a choice. Hear Him under those ancient olive trees: "My soul is exceedingly sorrowful, even to death. . . . If it is possible, let this cup pass from me; nevertheless not as I will, but as You will" (Matthew 26:38–39). Our Lord reached all the way into the depths of His own being and chose to follow not His own will, but the will of the One who had sent Him.

On our personal journey to Jerusalem, we will all come to the place in our own experience where we must choose God's will over our own.

CODE WORD: MENU

Today, as you look at a breakfast, lunch, or dinner menu, let it remind you that life is filled with choices. Make sure you choose God's will over your own. His way, His will, is always best.

A PASSION PROCLAMATION

Choose for yourselves this day whom you will serve. . . . As for me and my house, we will serve the LORD.

JOSHUA 24:15

Lord, today have Your will done in my life. Mold me. Make me according to Your will and not my own. In Jesus' name, amen.

One week after the bombing of Pearl Harbor, Franklin D. Roosevelt, in addressing the nation, said, "Those who have long enjoyed such privileges as we enjoy forget in time that men have died to win them."[5] Sadly, there is more truth than one might want to acknowledge in those words. During this season of Lent, we are reminded of the words of our Lord: "Greater love has no one than this, than to lay down one's life for his friends" (John 15:13).

When you think about it, freedom is never really free. It is always bought with blood. Jesus never fought in a war or marched in step in an army. He simply trudged up and down the dusty roads of Judea and the hills of Galilee, meeting needs, giving hope and comfort, healing broken bodies and wounded lives. You would think He must have been loved for those acts of kindness. But He wasn't. Instead, He was despised and rejected. He carried His own cross to His place of execution, and there the blessed Son of God, the heaven-sent manifestation of love, extended His already-beaten body on a cross and died for you and for me.

As we meditate on this "greater love" today, allow me the liberty to paraphrase Roosevelt's words: "We who have long enjoyed the spiritual privileges we enjoy must not forget that the Lord Jesus died to win them."

CODE WORD: FRIEND

Today, as you talk, text, email, or have lunch with a friend, let it be a reminder to you of Christ's supreme sacrifice. Yes, "greater love has no one than this, than to lay down one's life for his friends."

A PASSION PROCLAMATION

By this we know love, because He laid down His life for us.

1 John 3:16

Lord, You are the true Friend who "sticks closer than a brother."[6] May I never be counted among those who forget in time that You died for me. Amen.

G od proved His love toward us. He did not prove it by writing "I love you" in flaming letters across the sky. Instead, "in the fullness of time, God sent forth His Son" (Galatians 4:4). Jesus was no remedial action or some kind of last-minute splint for a broken world when all else had failed. He came right on time, and He "demonstrate[d] His own love toward us, in that while we were still sinners, Christ died for us" (Romans 5:8).

The phenomenal aspect of His love is that it was expressed not when we were perfect or deserving. He loved us "while we were still sinners." Think of that! And that is not all. The ultimate proof of His love toward us is that He "died for us." The price He paid to prove His love was great. Every lash of the whip across His back, every *thud* of the hammer driving spikes in His hands and feet, was the voice of God saying, "I love sinners."

I remember when our first child was born, holding her in my arms and thinking, *I would give her the world if I could.* Then the thought occurred to me that God had said just the opposite, "I will give My only Son to the world." No wonder the songwriter of old said, "Oh, the love that drew salvation's plan! Oh, the grace that brought it down to man . . . at Calvary."[7]

CODE WORD: THUMB

Today, when you wash your hands, look at your thumb and let it remind you that no one has a thumb print or DNA just like yours. You are an individual, indescribably loved by God. Let Him love you today.

A PASSION PROCLAMATION

For this reason I bow my knees to the Father of our Lord Jesus Christ, . . . that He would grant you . . . to know the love of Christ which passes knowledge, that you may be filled with all the fullness of God.

EPHESIANS 3:14–19

Lord, if You love me even in those moments when I am so unlovely, help me love those around me as You have loved me. In Jesus' name, amen.

DAY 18: WEDNESDAY

W hen Dr. R. G. Lee, the late, great preacher, first went on a Holy Land pilgrimage, he, along with his tour group, came to Golgotha, the place of the crucifixion. Lee, moved with emotion, ran ahead of the crowd. When the others arrived at that sacred spot, they found him on his knees, with tears streaming down his cheeks. "Oh, Dr. Lee," one of them exclaimed, "I see you have been here before."

"No," he replied. Then quickly correcting himself, he said, "Yes, I have. Two thousand years ago." Then came the words of Galatians 2:20: "I have been crucified with Christ, it is no longer I who live, but Christ lives in me."

As our Lord hung on the cross, the crowd saw only one man on the center cross. But the Father saw not just Christ but you and me and all others who would put their faith in Christ. When we come to Jesus, God takes our old life from us ("I have been crucified with Christ") and puts a new life in us ("Christ lives in me"). The Christian life is not a changed life. It is an exchanged life. You give Christ your old life, and He puts it away in the sea of His forgetfulness. And He gives you a brand-new life, a new life in Christ. It is an awesome thought: "Christ lives in me."

CODE WORD: LOGO

We love to identify with things. Certain logos tell the world the brand of clothing we are wearing. We proudly show our school colors and logos. Look at your key ring. Most likely it bears the logo of your automobile. When you look at a logo today, let it remind you of the privilege you have to identify with Jesus Christ. Let others see Him through the "logo" of your life and lips today.

A PASSION PROCLAMATION

I have been crucified with Christ; it is no longer I who live, but Christ lives in me; and the life which I now live in the flesh I live by faith in the Son of God, who loved me and gave Himself for me.

GALATIANS 2:20

Lord, speak through my mouth today; look at others through my eyes; live through me today so those with whom I come in contact will see You in me for Your glory. In Jesus' name, amen.

DAY 19: THURSDAY

I t has been said that leadership can be characterized by certain punctuation marks. Some think
leadership is characterized by the period, that is, the
command: "Go here. Do this. Do that." Others say
it is better characterized by the exclamation point,
expressing enthusiasm, expectancy, optimism. But
most often true leaders are characterized by that symbol that is bent in humility: the question mark. The
Lord Jesus was always asking questions. In fact, the
gospel accounts record more than one hundred questions escaping His lips. One day, at Caesarea Philippi,
He got to the heart of His own exclusivity when He
asked His disciples, "Who do *you* say that I am?"
(Matthew 16:15, emphasis added). Today He asks us
the same question. In fact, for each of us this Lenten
season, this is the question of eternity.

When asking this question in the language of the
New Testament, it is emphatic, that is, the "you" is
placed for emphasis at the beginning of the sentence.
It is as if Jesus were asking, "What about you? You
and you only? Who do *you* say that I am?" God bless
Simon Peter. We often bemoan his impulsiveness and
quick temper. But now he comes through: "You are
the Christ, the Son of the living God" (Matthew 16:16,

emphasis added). What do you say? This is a question you cannot avoid. Who do *you* say He is?

CODE WORD: TEMPERATURE

Today, when you check the temperature outside, let it remind you that scientific truth is narrow. Water freezes at 32 degrees Fahrenheit—not 33 or 34. That is narrow. How about math? 2 + 2 = 4 . . . not 3, not 7. So don't be surprised that theological truth is also narrow. Christ is the only way to eternal life. It is the very nature of truth: all truth is narrow.

A PASSION PROCLAMATION

"I am the way, the truth, and the life. No one comes to the Father except through Me."

JOHN 14:6

....

Lord, I believe that You are the one and only way to heaven, and I join Peter today in boldly acknowledging that YOU—and You alone—are the Christ, the Savior of the world. Amen.

Telling good news/bad news jokes was a part of growing up in our culture, like the pastor who stood up on Sunday to say, "The good news is we have enough money here this morning to pay off the church debt. But the bad news is, it is still in your pockets!"

When we come to Romans 6:23, we find some good news and some bad news. The bad news is "the wages of sin is death." We all find ourselves in this verse because the Bible says, "All have sinned and fall short of the glory of God" (Romans 3:23). A wage is what you get for doing something; it is something you have coming. Payday is coming someday. That is the bad news.

But the good news is this: "The gift of God is eternal life through Jesus Christ our Lord" (Romans 6:23b KJV). It is a gift . . . a free gift. It can't be earned nor is it deserved. It is yours to receive by faith. Jesus dealt with the bad news two thousand years ago when He *became* sin for us on the cross (2 Corinthians 5:21). Yes, the wages of sin is death. Jesus paid this price so we can finish the verse with the good news that forgiveness of sin and eternal life can be ours right now by accepting this God-provided gift by faith.

CODE WORD: NEWSPAPER

Today, when you pick up a newspaper or read an article online, let it remind you that in the midst of all the bad news, the good news can be found in Christ. And the headline reads, "Jesus Saves!"

A PASSION PROCLAMATION

The wages of sin is death; but the gift of God is eternal life through Jesus Christ our Lord.

ROMANS 6:23 KJV

....

Lord, no one has ever given me a gift as expressive and expensive as Your gift to me in Christ; not just abundant life here and now, but eternal life with You forever! Unworthy as I am, I receive this gift of Christ. In Jesus' name, amen.

DAY 21: SATURDAY

Along the journey to Jerusalem, Jesus came upon a colony of ten lepers isolated from everyone they knew and loved due to the contagious nature of their hideous disease. They shouted to Him for mercy as He passed by. He stopped, told them to go show themselves to the priests, and they were healed as they obeyed. They all were cleansed of their disease, but here the similarity ends.

Only "one of them . . . returned" (Luke 17:15) in thanksgiving. This leper, like the others, had a family to get back to, a business to tend to, but something was more pressing. We are not told his name. He belongs to that vast throng who live their beautiful lives and perform their selfless deeds in often anonymous ways. We may not know his name, but he is shouting to us today, "Get back to Jesus. Be grateful. Give thanks for all He has done for you."

Jesus looked at him and said, "Arise, go your way. Your faith has made you well" (Luke 17:19). Along your own journey to Jerusalem, remember that the God of this universe wants your thanks. And that is why the writer of Hebrews calls us to "continually offer the sacrifice of praise to God . . . giving thanks to His name" (13:15).

CODE WORD: RETURN

Today, when you return home from the office or from some appointment, let it remind you of the importance of returning daily to Jesus to simply say thanks for the wonderful things He has done and is doing in and through you.

A PASSION PROCLAMATION

Oh, give thanks to the LORD, for He is good! For His mercy endures forever.

PSALM 107:1

Lord, it is good to give thanks to You and to declare Your loving-kindness in the morning and Your faithfulness every night. Thank You for the realization that You are alive in me right now. In Jesus' name, amen.

Given the situation you may be facing with the seemingly inadequate resources at your disposal, you may be prone to ask what Andrew asked on a grassy, green hillside along the journey to Jerusalem: "What are they among so many?" (John 6:9). Throngs of people had gathered in Galilee to listen to Jesus, and hunger had set in. A small boy was found who had a sack lunch of a couple of fish and five barley loaves. Most of us know the story. Jesus multiplied the loaves and fishes, had the disciples feed thousands of people, and then had them take up the leftovers.

He was just a little lad with a little lunch. Maybe you feel as Andrew did that day, comparing the *little* you have with the *big* challenge in your life. But little always becomes much when you factor Christ into the equation of your life.

That boy left home that morning with the potential to feed thousands of people and didn't even know it! I wonder, *Is the same true with you?* You have incredible potential wrapped up in you to bless so many people today, and you may not even know it!

The boy in this story gave all, and that exchange tapped the eternal resources of heaven and brought them down into the bankrupt affairs of men. And Jesus is still at it today.

CODE WORD: LUNCH

Today as you eat lunch, let it remind you that God looks upon you not for who you are right now but for who you could be. Like the lad with the lunch, you are a person of huge potential.

A PASSION PROCLAMATION

For I know the thoughts that I think toward you, says the Lord, thoughts of peace and not of evil, to give you a future and a hope.

JEREMIAH 29:11

....

Lord, help me see myself as You see me today: as a person of promise, a person of potential to be used for Your good and Your glory. Take my life. Use me, Lord. In Jesus' name, amen.

Comfort zones . . . we all have them, and many of us never venture out from them. There are certain social, political, religious, and even economic comfort zones from which many of us seldom stray.

Jesus tells the story of a Samaritan, a member of a race despised by the Jews of His day, who came upon a fellow traveler along his way. The traveler had been beaten, robbed, and left bleeding on the side of the road. Some religious types had passed earlier and walked on by on the other side of the road, snuggled in their ecclesiastical garments and congratulating themselves for having never stooped so low as to attack an innocent traveler. But the Samaritan felt compassion, stopped, applied first aid, took the wounded man to an inn for extended care, and paid the bill (Luke 10:30–37).

Consider today the fact that you were that wounded man. Jesus saw you beaten by sin and lying on the side of the road. Overwhelmed by compassion and love for you, He left His own comfort zone of heaven, came into your world, clothed Himself in human flesh, and reached out to touch you. But that is not all! Like the Samaritan, He took you to a place of refuge, deposited you in His church, and promised that when He came back He would settle all accounts.

CODE WORD: POLITICS

When you read or hear of the politics of today, think about this: Do you just stay in your own comfort zones in life, only connecting with others who think like you and act like you? One of the things we learn as we follow Jesus is that comfort zones become obsolete when love enters the picture.

A PASSION PROCLAMATION

I can do all things through Christ who strengthens me.

PHILIPPIANS 4:13

....

Lord, Your Word says that I can do all things through You. Lead me in some way today to follow You out of my own comfort zone in order to be a blessing. Because if it is great to get a blessing, it is much greater to be a blessing. In Jesus' name, amen.

DAY 24: WEDNESDAY

Along the journey to His appointment with the cross in Jerusalem, Jesus often taught His followers spiritual truth in the form of parables, short allegorical stories designed to reveal deeper life lessons. The most familiar and often repeated of these is the parable of the prodigal son. It tells of a boy who came to his father, demanded his inheritance in advance, left home, and wasted it all in the bright lights of the big city. He ended up broke and working in a pigpen, feeding swine. Finally, he "came to himself," got up, returned home, and was welcomed into the loving and forgiving arms of his father and received a new beginning (Luke 15:11–32). Henry Wadsworth Longfellow referred to this parable as the greatest short story ever written.

We may call it the parable of the prodigal son, but Jesus' intentions were never for the boy to take center stage in the story. It is not about him. It is all about the father. Jesus begins the narrative saying, "A certain man had two sons" (v. 11). Read that sentence again. Who is the subject of the sentence? The father. He is the one on center stage. This is a story about the dad.

Along the journey to Jerusalem, Jesus was giving us a picture of our heavenly Father's unconditional love for you and me. He is standing on center stage, waiting . . . right now . . . to receive you back with open arms.

CODE WORD: WELCOME

When you use or hear this word today, let it remind you that God the Father has not abdicated His throne and is waiting with open arms to immerse you in His unconditional love.

A PASSION PROCLAMATION

Keep yourself in the love of God looking for the mercy of our Lord Jesus Christ unto eternal life.

Jude v. 21

Father, how great is Your unfailing love for me, so vast beyond all measure, that You should give Your only Son to make a wretch like me Your treasure. Thank You, Lord. Amen.

DAY 25: THURSDAY

When reading the parable of the prodigal son (Luke 15:11–32), we first see the father with an open hand. He let the boy go. Here is a dad wise enough to know that the way to keep his kids was to let them go and the way to lose them was to hold them too tight. He could have guilted the kid ("Are you trying to break your mother's heart?") or played the comparison game ("Why can't you be like your older brother?"), but he didn't. We see him here with an open hand, saying, "I release you." He let him go, but he never gave up on him.

Like the father in this story, your loving, heavenly Father has an open hand toward you. You are not a puppet. You are a person, with the ability to make decisions in life. And so, He lets you go . . . because the love you can voluntarily return to Him is indescribably valuable to Him. He may let you go your own way, and you may remove yourself from the environment of that love, but He will never stop loving you and never give up on you. He knows the way to keep you is to open His hands and release you.

CODE WORD: WASH

Today, as you wash your hands or look at your hands, let it remind you that God holds you in His hands today. He will never give up on you.

A PASSION PROCLAMATION

For I am persuaded that neither death nor life, nor angels nor principalities nor powers, nor things present nor things to come, nor height nor depth, nor any other created thing, shall be able to separate us from the love of God which is in Christ Jesus our Lord.

ROMANS 8:38–39

....

Lord, immerse me in Your love right now in this moment of quiet. I sense Your presence and abide in Your love. I do love You, Lord. In Jesus' name, amen.

M ost of us know the story well. The prodigal runs out of money and ends up with the menial task of feeding swine in a pigpen (not a very desirable job for a Jewish boy, I might add!). But he comes to himself and heads for home. Jesus said, "But when he was still a great way off, his father saw him and had compassion, and ran and fell on his neck and kissed him" (Luke 15:20). The boy came walking . . . but the father went running! His love that was tough enough to release his son was now tender enough to receive him. Look at their embrace . . . no crossed arms, pointed fingers, clenched fists; no cross-examination of "Where have you been?" or "Where is the money?" Just open arms. His open hands turn into open arms.

Along our own journey to Jerusalem, the Father is waiting for us with open arms. How grateful we can be during this season of Lent that God does not deal with us "according to our sins" or mistakes or failures but according to His tender mercies (Psalm 103:10). Is it time for you to "come to yourself" and return home to Him? When you do, you will find Him with open arms, saying, "I receive you."

CODE WORD: OPEN

As you go through the normal traffic patterns of your day, opening doors, opening drawers, opening letters, let each act be a reminder to you that the Father has open arms for you . . . no pointed fingers . . . no crossed arms . . . just open arms of forgiveness and a welcome home.

A PASSION PROCLAMATION

Love . . . does not seek its own, is not provoked, does not take into account a wrong suffered.

1 Corinthians 13:4–5 NASB

. . . .

Lord, thank You for the blood of Jesus, which provides covering for my sin. "Amazing love . . . how can it be?"[8] In Jesus' name, amen.

DAY 27: SATURDAY

The prodigal son returns home, and the party begins. Everyone is celebrating. The festivities are at a high point. But where is Dad? He is outside, attending to the older, obedient brother, who feels slighted by the scene inside. The father who opened his hands and opened his arms now opens his heart, assuring his older son of three important things:

- his presence: "Son, you are always with me" (Luke 15:31a);
- his provision: "All that I have is yours" (Luke 15:31b); and
- his purpose: "Your brother was dead and is alive, He was lost and is found" (Luke 15:32).

The most notable characteristic of this father—and our heavenly Father—is his transparency. He opened his heart to his children, saying, "I respect you."

Ironically, Jesus does not tell us how the story ends. Did the older boy go in and join the party? Did he stay outside sulking? We are never told. Perhaps the Lord ended the story and left it shrouded in silence so that you could complete the story today. And when you do, you will find a loving, heavenly Father not only with an open hand and open arms but with an open heart toward you, full of love, full of forgiveness.

CODE WORD: PRESENCE

Today you may be in the presence of many people at work, at play, and at home. Let this be a constant reminder to you that you have a Lord who says to you, "You are always with me" (Luke 15:31). Live today in the promise of His abiding presence. He will never leave you.

A PASSION PROCLAMATION

Let your conduct be without covetousness; be content with such things as you have. For He Himself has said, "I will never leave you nor forsake you."

HEBREWS 13:5

....

Lord, You are always with me . . . all You have is mine. Help me see the bigger picture of Your purpose for me and those around me today and rejoice in You and them. In Jesus' name, amen.

If you have ever memorized a verse of Scripture, most likely it is John 3:16: "For God so loved the world that He gave His only begotten Son, that whosoever believes in Him should not perish but have everlasting life." It is the verse most often heard in the simplicity and beauty of a little child's voice proudly reciting it from memory. And it is the verse most often whispered by aged saints as they breathe their last breaths. It is the entire gospel in a nutshell.

John 3:16 speaks of the *cause* of this great salvation: "For God so loved . . ." The single motivating factor behind God's entire redemptive plan is His love for you and me. This beloved verse also speaks of the *cost* of this salvation: "He gave His only Son." Jesus paid a high price to redeem us to Himself—death on a Roman cross outside the city gates of Jerusalem. And salvation's *condition*? "Whosoever believes in Him . . ." That speaks of me. It speaks of you. And any and all may come, placing their faith in Him alone. Finally, this verse speaks of salvation's *consequence*: We "shall not perish but have everlasting life." Those without Christ are perishing . . . a little more each day.

Let God love you today as you meditate on this old and oft-repeated promise.

CODE WORD: GIFT

What do you do to get a gift? You don't earn it or deserve it. Someone who loves you very much gives it freely to you, and all you have to do is receive it. God's gift of eternal life, although purchased at great expense, is a free gift. Your part? Receive it by faith.

A PASSION PROCLAMATION

The gift of God is eternal life in Jesus Christ our Lord.

ROMANS 6:23

. . . .

Lord, thank You for loving me even when I am so unloving. Your love has no boundaries. I receive Your unconditional love right now by faith. In Jesus' name, amen.

DAY 29: TUESDAY

Arguably, no one else's dying words have been more quoted or more memorable than those of Jesus of Nazareth. Nailed fast to a Roman cross, He spoke seven times. After a long night filled with betrayal and false arrest, lying testimonies and illegal trials, cruel mockery and a bloody scourging, Jesus' hands and feet were nailed to a cross, and it was dropped with a *thud* into a hole in the ground.

It was nine o'clock in the morning, and He hung on that instrument of death until noon, when a strange and mysterious darkness covered the earth for three hours. Shortly thereafter, He died. But before we mourn His death, take to heart His gracious dying words.

Jesus' first words from the cross were a prayer: "Father, forgive them, for they do not know what they do" (Luke 23:34). Jesus died praying for others. What He preached about loving enemies on a hillside in Galilee (Luke 6:28), He practiced on a cross on Golgotha.

Next came a promise to a man hanging near Him: "Today you will be with Me in paradise" (Luke 23:43). It is never too late for a new beginning.

Then, seeing His mother in the crowd, He pronounced to John, "Behold your mother!" and to His mother, "Woman, behold your son!" (John 19:26–27). Jesus gave John the responsibility of caring for His mother because He Himself was no longer Mary's Son; He was now her Savior!

CODE WORD: HAMMER

The next time you pick up a hammer to repair something in your home, let it remind you that Christ died an agonizing death, nailed fast to a Roman cross . . . for you.

A PASSION PROCLAMATION

"It is the Spirit who gives life; the flesh profits nothing. The words that I speak to you are spirit, and they are life."

JOHN 6:63

Lord, help me today to see others through Your eyes, even those who have spoken against me, and help me love them with Your amazing and unconditional love. In Jesus' name, amen.

For three hours total darkness enveloped the earth as Jesus hung on the cross. Darkness in the middle of the day! From the darkness came the piercing cry of the most haunting of all the words of Christ from the cross: "My God, My God, why have You forsaken Me?" (Matthew 27:46). This question has perplexed the minds of believers for centuries. Did a loving Father forsake His only Son in His greatest moment of need?

Many of us know far too well from our personal experiences the raw heartbreak that comes when we are forsaken by someone we love. Does God forsake His own? Did He forsake Shadrach, Meshach, and Abed-Nego in a fiery furnace (Daniel 3) or Daniel in a lions' den (Daniel 6)? No! Then why this strange cry escaping the bleeding lips of our Lord?

The prophet Habakkuk reminds us that God the Father is so holy He cannot look upon sin (Habakkuk 1:13). In the words of Isaiah, "All we like sheep have gone astray . . . and the LORD has laid on Him [Christ] the iniquity of us all" (Isaiah 53:6). On the cross Jesus took our iniquity, or sin, in His own body, suffering our shame, humiliation, agony, and death, all consequences we deserved. And for that period of time, the Father turned His face away, darkness enveloped the earth, and Jesus fought and won the battle of sin in our place. No wonder the Bible says, "Thanks be unto God for his unspeakable gift" (2 Corinthians 9:15 KJV).

CODE WORD: PRICE TAG

As you do your Easter shopping, let every price tag you see remind you that your salvation, although a free gift, came at an expensive price: the blood of Jesus Christ, God's Son.

A PASSION PROCLAMATION

[God] made [Jesus] who knew no sin to be sin for us, that we might become the righteousness of God in Him.

2 CORINTHIANS 5:21

. . . .

Lord, in the midst of this season of Lent, give me a glimpse of Your holiness. You are holy . . . set apart. And my own sin is so serious it necessitated the cross. Forgive me, Lord. In Jesus' name, amen.

DAY 31: THURSDAY

After the darkness two more words escaped Jesus' lips from the cross. The words heard by those around Him, now stunned by the mysterious and strange meteorological happenings of the day, were a request to meet His own physical need: "I thirst" (John 19:28). Here is a reminder of His own humanity. He was God, yes. But He was encased in a body of human flesh. He knew hunger, pain, thirst, emotions. He wept on occasion, and on others He laughed. Now, a simple plea. He was thirsty. But we should not fail to note that this cry of a personal need never came until after the battle of Calvary was fought and the darkness had turned back to light.

The next words came in rapid succession: "It is finished!" (John 19:30). The Greek word for "finished" here means that the debt is paid in full . . . your sin debt . . . mine . . . paid up, in full! Finished. Over. Done. Some seem to think that Jesus went to the cross and made a little down payment for our sin, and we have to work and earn our way the rest of the way home. No, never. He paid your sin debt in full. So much is behind that declaration, "It is finished!"

The last words from the cross were, "Father, into Your hands I commit My spirit" (Luke 23:46). And then He died!

CODE WORD: BILL

The next time you receive a bill for your mortgage, utilities, or credit card, let it be a reminder that you will never get a bill from Jesus. He paid off your account in full. Every sin for which you once owed is stamped with these words: PAID IN FULL!

A PASSION PROCLAMATION

You were not redeemed with corruptible things,
like silver or gold, from your aimless conduct
received by tradition from your fathers, but
with the precious blood of Christ, as of a
lamb without blemish and without spot.

1 PETER 1:18–19

. . . .

Lord, I am learning it is all about grace, Your marvelous, matchless grace. A simple thank-You seems so inadequate. Take my life and make it useful to You. In Jesus' name, amen.

DAY 32: FRIDAY

The consensus of sociology confirms that the number one quest in life for most men and women is a search for a meaningful relationship in life. Many have never known even one. The younger generations are the products of a massive divorce rate in our culture, and many of them are homesick for a home they have never known. Truly meaningful relationships are few and far between. Thus, many young adults are on a search . . . desirous of just one meaningful relationship to enjoy.

Paul reminds us that "in Him [Christ] we have redemption through His blood, the forgiveness of sins, according to the riches of His grace" (Ephesians 1:7). Note those first two words: "In Him." What Christ has to offer is not a religion or a ritual but a vibrant and meaningful relationship in Him.

There are only three types of relationships in life: outward (your relationships with others), inward (your relationship with yourself), and upward (your relationship with God through Jesus Christ). And the bottom line? We will never be properly related to others until we are properly related to ourselves, and this will never happen until we discover how valuable we are to God and come into a relationship with Him by placing our trust in Christ alone. The very thing for which we are searching—a meaningful relationship—can only be found "in *Him*."

CODE WORD: MIRROR

When you look at yourself in the mirror today, let it be a reminder to you of the three types of relationships and the fact that you will never find true self-worth until you begin with a personal relationship with Christ. No wonder the Bible says, "Christ *in you*, the hope of glory" (Colossians 1:27, emphasis added).

A PASSION PROCLAMATION

But as many as received Him, to them He gave the right to become children of God, to those who believe in His name.

JOHN 1:12

. . . .

Lord, help me see clearly today that I will never be properly related to others on a horizontal level until I am properly related to You in a vertical dimension. In Jesus' name, amen.

DAY 33: SATURDAY

My wife, Susie, and I are fortunate enough to own a home and a car. Some time ago we had to replace some eaves along the roof line, not because the roof was leaking, but because we noted some rot in the wood. Periodically we take our car in for an inspection even though it is running smoothly. We call it "preventive maintenance." Most of what goes wrong with my house or car does so because of one word—*neglect*. Neglect has adverse effects on physical things, but it is much more dangerous in the spiritual realm.

The writer of Hebrews asks a probing question—"How shall we escape if we neglect so great a salvation?" (2:3). As we come now to the door of Holy Week, there are three responses people give to the gospel. Some accept it. Some reject it. But most simply neglect it.

While many do not accept by faith the claims of Christ, most do not flat-out reject them either. Perhaps you, or someone you know, is among that vast throng of people who simply neglect Christ's continual call, deceived into thinking there will always be adequate time to name Jesus as Lord and Savior. The reality is, you will either accept Him or reject Him, for not to decide is to decide!

CODE WORD: CHOICE

As you go through this day, you are faced with one choice after another . . . where to eat lunch, what to order, and so on. Let each decision be a reminder that the greatest choice we can ever make is accepting Jesus Christ as our personal Lord and Savior. If you have not done that, what are you waiting for?

A PASSION PROCLAMATION

I have set before you life and death, the blessing and the curse. So choose life in order that you may live.

DEUTERONOMY 30:19

Lord, thank You for giving me free will to make choices in life. I am not a puppet. I am a person in Your image. Help me choose Your will and Your way this day. In Jesus' name, amen.

DAY 34: PALM SUNDAY

Palm Sunday was filled with crowds and shouts of hosanna, a parade, if you please, along with a pep rally on the Mount of Olives. But that was all a sham. And our Lord knew it. Within a few short days the crowd would disappear, and their cheers would be turned into jeers. Can you picture Jesus riding over palm branches on the back of a donkey to the loud praises of the people? He was the center of attention. He must have been smiling from ear to ear, waving at the masses. But look closer. The Bible tells us that when He saw the city, He "wept over it." Through His tears we can hear His words: "If you had known . . . the things that make for your peace. But now they are hidden from your eyes" (Luke 19:41–42).

Those Jerusalem crowds wanted a military leader to put down the Roman oppression. And when they realized they were not getting what they wanted, they crowned Him a king, all right, but with thorns.

And so our Lord sat on the Mount of Olives and wept. He cried. Tears welled up in His eyes, flowed down His bronze cheeks into His beard. Is this Man of Sorrows still weeping today, troubled by our own blinded eyes?

CODE WORD: TEARS

Jesus is still weeping today. Does He weep *with* you, touched by your broken heart? Or does He weep *over* you, troubled by your blinded eyes?

A PASSION PROCLAMATION

God is our refuge and strength, a very present help in time of trouble.... Be still, and know that I am God.

PSALM 46:1, 10

....

Lord, those two words of Palm Sunday are power-ful and pointed: "He wept." You cried. Tears have a language all their own. Thank You for the gift of tears. In Jesus' name, amen.

DAY 35: MONDAY

Holy Week had a strange beginning. Throngs of people had made their way to Jerusalem for the annual Passover pilgrimage to offer their sacrifices at the temple. Those with little financial means would purchase smaller animals, such as turtledoves, for their offerings. These would be bought inside the temple compound. Because it was unlawful to purchase such an offering with Roman coins, the religious leaders had set up a system whereby they would charge exorbitant prices, shrewdly cheating the poor who were forced to buy in this monopoly.

Upon entering the Temple Mount, Jesus witnessed this disgusting display and proceeded to turn over the tables of the money changers and drive them out of the temple area, shouting that they had turned this holy "house of prayer" into "a den of thieves" (Mark 11:17). Their sin was not in selling sacrifices for temple worship but in perpetrating fraud and deceit out of greed. They had forgotten an important truth: God always comes down on the side of the poor.

Jesus Himself lived with a special affinity for the poor. He was born in the most impoverished circumstances imaginable, and when He was buried, it was in a borrowed tomb. The more we become like Him, the more we will love justice and take a stand for the wounded, the ignored, and the exploited who are all around us.

CODE WORD: MONEY

Today, as you exchange money in the regular enterprises of your day, allow each exchange to remind you of the importance of standing where Jesus always stood, "at the right hand of the poor" (Psalm 109:31).

A PASSION PROCLAMATION

What does the LORD require of you but to do justly, to love mercy, and to walk humbly with your God?

MICAH 6:8

....

Lord, may my own heart be Your temple today, cleansed from sin by Your presence in my life. Purify my motives and desires today for Your own glory. In Jesus' name, amen.

DAY 36: TUESDAY

I t is impossible to imagine the pain, the grief, the sorrow Christ endured in dying such a slow, agonizing death. The writer of Hebrews reminds us that it was "for the joy that was set before Him" that Jesus "endured the cross, despising the shame" (12:2).

Shame is a dreadful emotion. Our Lord was stripped naked . . . *naked* . . . before all the onlookers. He was then beaten like a common criminal and finally nailed to a cross. He endured the physical shame, the emotional shame, and what was worse, the spiritual shame as the Father turned away His face from all the vile sinfulness Jesus was bearing in His own body on the cross. Jesus, the heaven-sent Messenger of love, the beloved and only begotten Son of the Father, had to suffer not only the guilt but the shame of the sin of the entire world . . . murderers, molesters, racists, and oppressors of the poor.

Nine hundred years ago, an isolated monk, Bernard of Clairvaux, framed it best:

> *O sacred Head, now wounded,*
> *With grief and shame weighed down.*
> *Now scornfully surrounded, with thorns, thine only*
> *   crown. . . .*
> *How art thou pale with anguish, with sore abuse*
> *   and scorn!*

*How does thy visage languish, which once was
  bright as morn![9]*

Go to the cross today. Stay there for a while. Jesus'
death deserves our serious reflection.

CODE WORD: PAIN

Today let every ache, every pain, be a reminder of how
much more Jesus suffered, enduring the cross and
"despising the shame" . . . for you.

A PASSION PROCLAMATION

*I gave My back to those who struck Me, and My
cheeks to those who plucked out the beard; I did
not hide My face from shame and spitting.*

ISAIAH 50:6

· ·

*Lord, saying thank-You for the cross seems so
inadequate. I seek to understand what Your death
means to me. Your love is unfathomable, and Your
mercy has no end. In Jesus' name, amen.*

Have you noticed how a particular smell can bring instant memory recall of a particular place or a particular person from the past? It can be a powerful reminder of an event decades after it happened. One of my high school teachers wore a fragrance called "Jungle Gardenia." It had a distinctive smell that would linger in a room long after she had left it. To this day when I get a whiff of it, my mind immediately races back to her.

Fragrance takes center stage in the story of Mary of Bethany. Along with her siblings, Martha and Lazarus, she was a devoted follower of Jesus of Nazareth. On one occasion Jesus, along with other invited guests, joined them in their home for a dinner party. After dinner Mary did an astonishing thing. She brought some very expensive and precious oil and poured it out on Jesus' feet. While some rebuked her for not selling it and giving the money to the poor, Jesus blessed her for this extravagant act of worship. Then John, who was sitting at the table with them, recorded, "The [whole] house was filled with the fragrance of the oil" (John 12:3).

Mary's gift became a blessing to everyone in the home that night who got caught up in its sweet fragrance. A life fully devoted to the Lord will have a lingering effect of His own sweet fragrance.

CODE WORD: FRAGRANCE

Today, when you inhale a certain fragrance, let it be a reminder to you of the importance of leaving behind the fragrance of Jesus wherever you go, "a sweet-smelling aroma . . . well pleasing to God" (Philippians 4:18).

A PASSION PROCLAMATION

For we are to God the fragrance of Christ among those who are being saved and among those who are perishing.

2 CORINTHIANS 2:15

....

Lord, may my conversation and conduct be such that when I walk away from others today, the sweet fragrance of Your presence will remain. In Jesus' name, amen.

DAY 38: THURSDAY

Thursday was a busy day. The disciples were hastily gathering the food and supplies necessary for the seder meal, not to mention trying to secure a room for the dinner. All was in order when they gathered on Mount Zion that fateful evening. And then they got into an argument, right there at the table. About what? Who of them would be the greatest in the coming kingdom Jesus had promised! At this point the greatest among them became the servant of all of them. Jesus arose from the table, girded Himself with a towel, and knelt before each of them to wash their feet. Whose feet needed washing the most that night? Whose feet in a matter of hours would be nailed fast to a Roman cross? And His were the only feet that left that night unwashed.

At the end of the meal, they sang a hymn and retreated beneath the olive trees of Gethsemane's garden to pray. Judas came in the shadows, followed by a mob with torches, and planted the kiss of betrayal on Jesus' cheek. Jesus called him "Friend" (Matthew 26:50). To be attacked by the enemy is one thing, but to be betrayed by one of your closest "friends" is quite another.

Before we are quick to point a finger of accusation at Judas, or Peter, or any of the others who betrayed Jesus that night . . . we must ask ourselves on this solemn day of Holy Week, "Lord, is it I?" (Matthew 26:22).

CODE WORD: RELATIONSHIPS

When you think about a good friend today or interact with a group of friends at lunch or dinner, let it remind you that you have a true Friend, the Lord Jesus, who always "sticks closer than a brother" (Proverbs 18:24). Holy Week is not about rituals or religion. It is about a relationship with Jesus.

A PASSION PROCLAMATION

No longer do I call you servants, for a servant does not know what his master is doing; but I have called you friends, for all things that I heard from My Father I have made known to you.

JOHN 15:15

Lord, I am no better than Judas. I may not have betrayed You for thirty pieces of silver, but I am too often quick to turn from my loyalty to You. May Your goodness, like a fetter, bind my wandering heart to You this day. In Jesus' name, amen.

DAY 39: GOOD FRIDAY

At some time or another, most of us have been caught in a "Freudian slip," an inadvertent mistake in speech revealing an unconscious thought of some kind. This is closely akin to the "double entendre," a particular way of saying something that has a double meaning.

Having stripped Jesus naked, beaten Him with a whip, and battered His head with a reed, His enemies began to mock and spit upon Him. Then a Roman soldier spewed out sarcastically, "Hail, King of the Jews!" (Mark 15:18). They even nailed a sign over His head, stating, "THIS IS JESUS THE KING OF THE JEWS" (Matthew 27:37). Meaning this as a cruel joke, these soldiers unwittingly never spoke or wrote greater truth. He was a King, all right, but His kingdom was not of this world. He came to rule over the human heart . . . not on some earthly throne.

A few hours later, the religious types added their ignorance to the barrage of double entendres around the cross: "He saved others, Himself He cannot save" (Matthew 27:42). Unknowingly, they blurted out for all posterity the substitutionary aspect of Jesus' death. He could not save Himself and save us at the same time.

And who of us can forget the thief hanging next

to Him? "If You are the Christ, save Yourself." Then quickly he added, "And us!" (Luke 23:39). Jesus could not do both. He died so we might be saved.

CODE WORD: SOVEREIGN

Let these three sayings, embedded in the larger story of the cross, remind you today of God's sovereignty over the events of Holy Week. He was in total control. Marvel at this, because you are a part of this story too.

A PASSION PROCLAMATION

*For the Lord is a great God, and the
great King above all gods.*

Psalm 95:3, emphasis added

....

Lord, thank You for bearing in my place not only the pain and suffering but also the mockery and ridicule that accompanied it. Reign today as Lord on the throne of my heart. In Your name I pray. Amen.

DAY 40: SATURDAY

Saturday. Silence. Jesus had died. He was in a sealed tomb. His disciples and followers were beyond exhaustion, numb with sorrow and disappointment. They had forsaken Him and fled in the hour of His deepest need. In the utter despair of the moment, they exclaimed, "We were hoping that it was He who was going to redeem Israel" (Luke 24:21).

It was the Jewish sabbath, the day of rest from labor, a day of silent reflection. The death of dreams and hopes is not an easy one to endure. What confusion and fear must have been racing through the disciples' minds.

On this day consider these poignant words reflecting such profound truth:

> *Alas! and did my Savior bleed, and did*
> *   my Sovereign die?*
> *Would He devote that sacred Head for*
> *   sinners such as I?*
> *Was it for sins that I have done, He*
> *   suffered on the tree?*
> *Amazing pity! Grace unknown! And*
> *   love beyond degree.*
> *But drops of grief can never repay the*
> *   debt of love I owe.*

Here, Lord, I give myself away,
It's all that I can do.[10]

Yes, it is Saturday, but don't give up hope. Something *big* is about to happen . . . Sunday is coming!

CODE WORD: WAIT

Today, be patient when you have to wait on something or someone. Let it remind you that "weeping may endure for a night, but joy comes in the morning" (Psalm 30:5).

A PASSION PROCLAMATION

But those who wait on the LORD shall renew their strength; they shall mount up with wings like eagles.

ISAIAH 40:31

....

Lord, when common sense says my situation is hopeless, give me the uncommon sense to believe that You still have Your own ways of making the impossible possible. In Jesus' name, amen.

EASTER SUNDAY

E aster morning. You can almost smell the fresh-
ness of that cool Middle Eastern sunrise. The
women arrive at the tomb early only to find that it
is empty! Then they are startled by an angelic being
informing them the Lord is not there but that He is
risen. Then the angel says, "Go, tell His disciples—
and Peter—that He is going before you into Galilee"
(Mark 16:7, emphasis added).

One might have expected the angel to say, "Go,
tell the disciples—and Pilate," or Herod, or any of
the others who played a part in Jesus' indictment. Or,
"Go, tell the disciples—and John." After all, John was
the lone disciple standing at the foot of the cross that
Friday. But our Lord knew Peter's heart. He was the
one who had so blatantly denied Christ in the hour of
testing and was in dire need of a word of encourage-
ment, a new beginning, a second chance. These two
words make all the difference: "and Peter"!

This is the message of Easter. Many of us are in
need of a second chance on this day. Perhaps you, too,
have faced your own setbacks or sorrows. Perhaps you
need these two little words on this Easter morning:
"Go, tell the disciples—*and* [put your name here]."
One failure doesn't make a flop. Easter means a new
start, a new life, a new beginning. This is the day that

reveals that the second chance is not only possible but profitable . . . as Peter found out.

CODE WORD: BASEBALL

One of the things this spring season brings is the sound of the cracking of the bat as baseball season begins. Let this be a reminder that even though you might strike out, you get to bat again! Easter is the message of the second chance.

A PASSION PROCLAMATION

But this I call to mind, and therefore I have hope: the steadfast love of the Lord never ceases; his mercies never come to an end; they are new every morning; great is your faithfulness.

LAMENTATIONS 3:21–23 ESV

Lord, I thank You that no matter what I may have done . . . or not done, the blood of Jesus Christ cleanses me from all sin and provides for me a second chance. Your love never ceases, and Your mercies know no end. In Jesus' name, amen.

EPILOGUE

Along our "journey to Jerusalem," we have heard a lot of words from the lips of our Lord. As I have been devotionally reading the Gospels during these days on my personal journey, I have found myself time and again longing to have a visual recording of Jesus' words instead of just having them emerge from the printed pages of Scripture. How did He say what He said? Where did He put the inflection in the questions He asked?

There is no more personal question than the one He asked at the tomb of Lazarus. Having declared His deity, saying, "I am the resurrection and the life. He who believes in Me . . . shall never die," He turned to His hearers and asked, "Do you believe this?" (John 11:25–26). This is Easter's bottom-line question: Do you believe this? How enlightening it would be if we could watch a video of this.

Perhaps He asked, "Do *you* believe this?" When it comes to saving faith in the finished work of Christ, what matters is not what anyone else believes. It is intensely personal.

It may be that He asked it like this: "Do you *believe* this?" He is not interested in whether you give intellectual assent to His claims. Jesus wants to know if you put your total trust and faith in what He says. The real issue is one of faith. Easter's bottom-line question is not only personal; it is pointed.

Finally, we come to the heart of the issue. Saving faith rests on objective truth and fact. It could well be Jesus placed His emphasis on the last word in the question—"Do you believe *this*?" The question follows on the heels of an amazing claim: "I am the resurrection and the life. He who believes in Me, though he may die, he shall live. And whoever lives and believes in Me shall never die. Do you believe *this*?" (John 11:25–26, emphasis added).

Do you? Do you believe this claim about His deity? The fundamental belief of the Christian faith is that Jesus of Nazareth is God Himself, "the image of the invisible God . . . All things were created through Him and for Him" (Colossians 1:15–16). Do you believe His claim about your destiny? "Though he may die, he shall live" (John 11:25). Your body will one day die, but not your spirit. There is a part of you that will live as long as God lives, which is forever and ever.

There are a lot of big questions that come our way in life. But there is only one question that will matter in death: "Do *you* believe this?" You can settle the question once and for all by responding, "Yes, Lord, I believe that You are the Christ, the Son of God" (John 11:27).

If this is the desire of your heart, the following is a prayer you can pray.

Dear Lord Jesus,

I know I have sinned and am undeserving of eternal life. Please forgive me. Thank You for taking all my sin upon Your own self and dying on the cross in my place, suffering the very death I deserved. I trust that You are the One and only One who can save me from eternal separation from a holy God. So I invite You now to be the Lord and King of my life. I turn my face to You, accepting Your gracious gift of eternal life and offer of total forgiveness. Thank You, Lord, for coming into my life to live as my personal Savior and Lord. I believe! In Your name I pray. Amen.

A simple prayer can never save you, but Jesus can, and will, if this prayer has expressed the desire of your heart. You can now claim the promise Jesus made to all who would follow Him: "Most assuredly . . . he who believes in Me has everlasting life" (John 6:47).

You are now ready to begin the great adventure for which you were created in the first place: to know Christ and to walk with Him daily on your own "journey to the New Jerusalem."

ENDNOTES

DAY 3: SATURDAY
1. James Weldon Johnson, *God's Trombones: Seven Negro Sermons in Verse* (New York: Penguin Classics, 2008), 15.

DAY 6: WEDNESDAY
2. Ephesians 3:20.

DAY 7: THURSDAY
3. William Cowper, "There Is a Fountain," 1772.

DAY 8: FRIDAY
4. Harry D. Clarke, "Into My Heart," 1924.

DAY 16: MONDAY
5. Franklin D. Roosevelt, Proclamation 2524—Bill of Rights Day, November 27, 1941, American Presidency Project website, http://www.presidency.ucsb.edu/ws/?pid=16046.
6. Proverbs 18:24.

DAY 17: TUESDAY
7. William Newell, "At Cavalry," 1895.

DAY 26: FRIDAY
8. Charles Wesley, "And Can It Be?" 1738.

DAY 36: TUESDAY
9. Bernard of Clairvaux, "O Sacred Head, Now Wounded," 1153.

DAY 40: SATURDAY
10. Isaac Watts, "At the Cross," 1707.

MISSION:DIGNITY

All the author's royalties and any additional proceeds from the Code series (including *The Christmas Code*) go to the support of Mission:Dignity, a ministry that enables thousands of retired ministers (and in most cases their widows) who are living near the poverty level to live out their days with dignity and security. Many of them spent their ministries in small churches that were unable to provide adequately for their retirement. They also lived in church-owned parsonages and had to vacate them upon their vocational retirement as well. Mission:Dignity tangibly shows these good and godly servants they are not forgotten and will be cared for in their declining years.

All the expenses for this ministry are paid for out of an endowment that has already been raised. Consequently, anyone who gives to Mission:Dignity can be assured that every cent of their gift goes straight to one of these precious saints in need.

Find out more by visiting www.guidestone.org and clicking on the Mission:Dignity icon, or call toll-free at 888-984-8433.

TRANSFORM YOUR HEART WITH

God's Word

The Joshua Code is designed to walk you through a year-long journey of meditating on one verse a week in order to recall and recite Scripture at will. Topics include temptation, understanding salvation, prayer, grace, vision, integrity, and more.

The Jesus Code takes you on a journey with one critical question each week to study and meditate on until the answer is firmly fixed in your mind and heart. Those answers will show God's will for your life, and they will help you feel confident as you share your faith with others.

The James Code challenges readers to give feet to their faith with applicable truth from the book of James emphasizing that an effective Christian life is not about faith and works, but is about faith that works.

100% of the author's royalties and proceeds goes to support Mission:Dignity—a ministry providing support for impoverished retired pastors and missionaries.

THOMAS NELSON
Since 1798

LEARN TO BE EFFECTIVE

culture warriors

In *The Daniel Code*, Daniel steps off the pages of Scripture and into our modern culture today to reveal some timeless principles—a sort of "Daniel Code"—that enable you to not simply exist in our culture but to engage it and survive it as well. You will discover that the same God who ensured Daniel's victories is here for you today.

The Believer's Code invites readers into a 365-day journey. Adapted from *The Joshua Code*, *The Jesus Code*, *The James Code*, and *The Daniel Code*, as well as brand-new applications and takeaways for readers, includes a short devotional reading, scripture, and a Code Word for each day, along with a challenge to put their faith in practice.

The Nehemiah Code Who is not in need of new beginning? Whether it be broken relationships, integrity missteps, or loss, most of us will spend some or much of the next year trying to restore something. The good news is . . . it's never too late for a new beginning.

100% of the author's royalties and proceeds goes to support Mission:Dignity—a ministry providing support for impoverished retired pastors and missionaries.

THOMAS NELSON
Since 1798